PowerPhonics™

My Birthday

Learning the IR Sound

Susan Hogenkamp

The Rosen Publishing Group's
PowerKids Press™
New York

It is my birthday. This is my birthday party.

Girls come to my birthday party.

Boys come to my birthday party.

HAPPY
BIRTHDAY

First we eat birthday cake.

Then we play birthday games.

I get a shirt for my birthday.

I get a toy giraffe for my birthday.

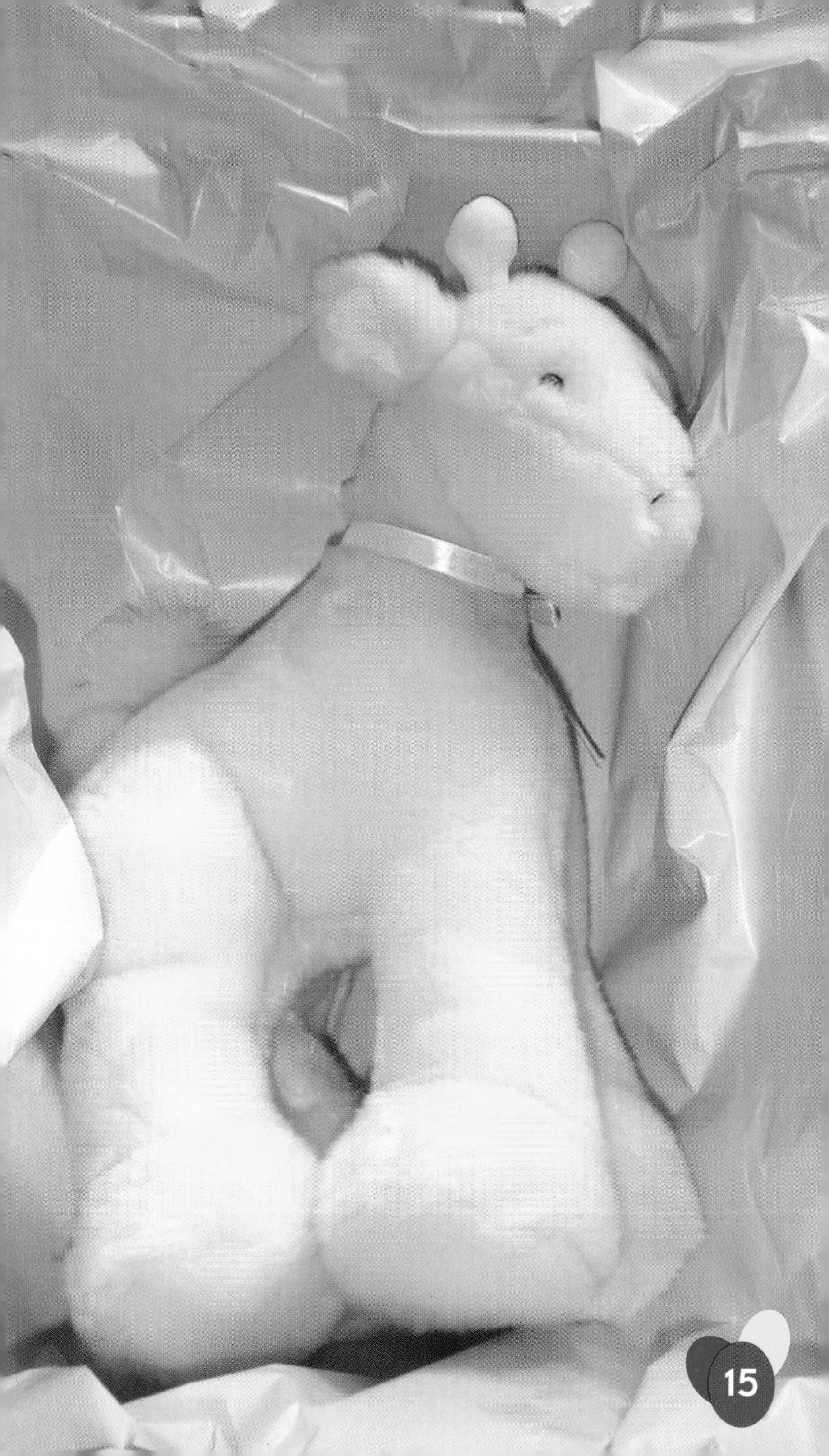

I get a bird for my birthday.

We go to the circus for my birthday.

I have fun on my birthday!

Word List

bird
birthday
circus
first
giraffe
girls
shirt

Instructional Guide

Note to Instructors:
One of the essential skills that enable a young child to read is the ability to associate letter-sound symbols and blend these sounds to form words. Phonics instruction can teach children a system that will help them decode unfamiliar words and, in turn, enhance their word-recognition skills. We offer a phonics-based series of books that are easy to read and understand. Each book pairs words and pictures that reinforce specific phonetic sounds in a logical sequence. Topics are based on curriculum goals appropriate for early readers in the areas of science, social studies, and health.

Letters/Sound: ir – Pronounce and write words that have the **ir** sound in them, such as the following: *bird, birthday, dirt, girl, shirt, first, third.* Ask the child to underline **ir** in each word. Have the child think of sentences for each **ir** word.

Phonics Activities:
- Give definitions of **ir** words, such as those below. Have the child name the words defined and tell their beginning and ending sounds: *the opposite of boy (girl), it comes after second when you're counting (third), needing a drink (thirsty), not clean (dirty), at the head of the line (first), an animal with feathers (bird), a round shape (circle), a show with clowns, acrobats, and animals (circus).*
- Have the child name the **ir** words they hear in the following sentences: *The girl next door is in third grade. We got our shirts dirty playing baseball. We went to the circus on Mom's birthday.*
- Provide the child with a set of consonant cards and several **ir** cards. Pronounce one-syllable words having the **ir** sound. Have the child form them with their cards.

Additional Resources:
- Hutchins, Pat. *Happy Birthday, Sam.* New York: Morrow Avon, 1991.
- Running Press Book Publishers Staff. *The Birthday Box: A Gift of Good Wishes, to Unlock & Treasure.* Philadelphia, PA: Running Press Book Publishers, 1997.

Published in 2002 by The Rosen Publishing Group, Inc.
29 East 21st Street, New York, NY 10010

Book Design: Haley Wilson

Photo Credits: Cover © Bill Tucker/International Stock; pp. 3, 9, 19, 21 © SuperStock; p. 5 © Dennie Cody/FPG International; p. 7 © VCG/FPG International; p. 11 © Eric Pearle/FPG International; pp. 13, 15 by Haley Wilson; p. 17 © Australia Picture Library/Index Stock.

Library of Congress Cataloging-in-Publication Data

Hogenkamp, Susan.
My birthday : learning the IR sound / Susan Hogenkamp.
p. cm. — (Power phonics/phonics for the real world)
ISBN 0-8239-5948-1 (lib. bdg.)
ISBN 0-8239-8293-9 (pbk.)
6-pack ISBN 0-8239-9261-6
1. Children's parties—Juvenile literature. 2. Birthdays—Juvenile literature. [1. Birthdays. 2. Parties. 3. English language—Phonetics.]
I. Title. II. Series.
GV1205 .H59 2001
394.2—dc21

2001000839

Manufactured in the United States of America